The Worship Leader's Guide to
CALLING ON GOD

Inclusive Christian Prayers for Three Years of Sundays

Peter Bankson & Deborah Sokolove

Other Prayer and Worship Resources from SkyLight Paths

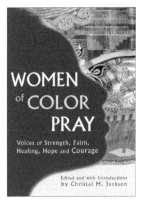

Women of Color Pray
Voices of Strength, Faith, Healing, Hope and Courage
Edited and with Introductions by Christal M. Jackson

This beautiful collection of prayers will take you on a journey into the spiritual walk of women of color around the world—including Asia, the Middle East and Africa—as well as Native American, African American, Asian American and Hispanic women in the United States.

5 x 7¼, 208 pp, Paperback, 978-1-59473-077-1

Men Pray
Voices of Strength, Faith, Healing, Hope and Courage
By the Editors at SkyLight Paths
Introductions by Brian D. McLaren

This collection celebrates the profound variety of ways men around the world have called out to the Divine—with words of joy, praise, gratitude, wonder, petition and even anger.

5 x 7¼, 192 pp, Hardcover, 978-1-59473-395-6

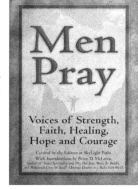

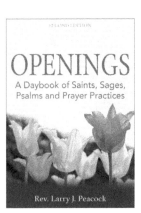

Openings, 2nd Edition
A Daybook of Saints, Sages, Psalms and Prayer Practices
By Rev. Larry J. Peacock

A prayerbook for every day of the year, with ancient and modern sages from inside and outside the Christian tradition and a wide variety of spiritual practices and reflections for every season.

6 x 9, 448 pp, Paperback, 978-1-59473-545-5

Sacred Attention
A Spiritual Practice for Finding God in the Moment
By Margaret D. McGee

Accessible, humorous and meaningful reflections and practices to help you deepen your awareness of yourself and your relationship to all that is around you—and within you.

6 x 9, 144 pp, Paperback, 978-1-59473-291-1; Hardcover, 978-1-59473-232-4

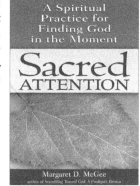

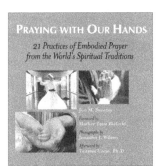

Praying with Our Hands
21 Practices of Embodied Prayer from the World's Spiritual Traditions
By Jon M. Sweeney
Photographs by Jennifer J. Wilson
Foreword by Mother Tessa Bielecki
Afterword by Taitetsu Unno, PhD

A spiritual guidebook for bringing prayer into our bodies, with twenty-one simple ways of using our hands to speak to God, presented in word and image.

8 x 8, 96 pp, 22 b/w photos, Paperback, 978-1-893361-16-4

Lectio Divina—The Sacred Art
Transforming Words & Images into Heart-Centered Prayer
By Christine Valters Paintner, PhD

Break open this ancient contemplative practice of listening deeply for God's voice in sacred texts—and expand your practice to include sacred reading of the world through image, sound, nature and life experience.

5½ x 8½, 240 pp, Paperback, 978-1-59473-300-0

CALLING ON GOD

Inclusive Christian Prayers for Three Years of Sundays

Worship Leader's Guide

Peter Bankson & Deborah Sokolove

CHRISTIAN JOURNEYS
FROM SKYLIGHT PATHS® PUBLISHING
Sunset Farm Offices, Route 4, P.O. Box 237, Woodstock, VT 05091
Tel: (802) 457-4000 Fax: (802) 457-40041
www.skylightpaths.com
www.christianjourneysbooks.com

Calling on God: Inclusive Christian Prayers for Three Years of Sundays—Worship Leader's Guide

2014 Paperback Edition, First Printing
© 2014 by Peter Bankson and Deborah Sokolove

For information regarding permission to reprint material from this book, please mail or fax your request in writing to SkyLight Paths Publishing, Permissions Department, at the address / fax number listed below, or email your request to permissions@skylightpaths.com.

10 9 8 7 6 5 4 3 2 1

Manufactured in the United States of America
Cover design: Michael Myers
Cover art: Deborah Sokolove

SkyLight Paths Publishing is creating a place where people of different spiritual traditions come together for challenge and inspiration, a place where we can help each other understand the mystery that lies at the heart of our existence.

SkyLight Paths sees both believers and seekers as a community that increasingly transcends traditional boundaries of religion and denomination—people wanting to learn from each other, *walking together, finding the way.*

SkyLight Paths, "Walking Together, Finding the Way" and colophon are trademarks of LongHill Partners, Inc., registered in the U.S. Patent and Trademark Office.

Walking Together, Finding the Way
Published by SkyLight Paths Publishing
A Division of LongHill Partners, Inc.
Sunset Farm Offices, Route 4, P.O. Box 237
Woodstock, VT 05091
Tel: (802) 457-4000 Fax: (802) 457-4004
www.skylightpaths.com

Contents

A Typical Order of Service for Seekers Church

We hope the prayers in *Calling on God* are a blessing to you and your worshiping community. Below is an annotated basic order of worship for Seekers Church to give you an idea of how the prayers in *Calling on God* fit into our overall worship. Using this outline, Celebration Circle writes a new order of worship for each season.

GATHERING

An informal thirty-minute gathering outside the sanctuary provides an opportunity to share news, welcome visitors, celebrate birthdays, and make announcements about activities of interest to community members. At the conclusion of Gathering Time, a member offers a prayer for peace and justice, lights a candle, and leads the congregation upstairs to continue worship in the sanctuary.

Entrance

We enter the sanctuary in silence, to continue our worship with a time of reflection. There is a visual composition on the altar table beneath the life-sized empty cross. These images and the bulletin covers relate to the worship theme for the season. There is also a reading in the liturgy for silent reflection during this time. Like the composition on the altar, these readings nurture reflection on the worship theme for the season. This initial time for reflection includes music chosen to complement the sermon and members of the community lighting candles on the altar table. This is often an opportunity for our children to help lead us in worship.

Call to Worship

We open our worship with an invitation to bring ourselves—spirit, mind, and body—into the presence of God with a call to worship meant to remind all of us that we are among God's beloved, welcomed into the body of the risen Christ. Here is a sample Easter call to worship, written by the Celebration Circle:

Leader: Christ is risen!

People: Christ is risen indeed! Alleluia!

Leader: We come to retell the ancient stories,
 to restore our dreams and hopes for new beginnings.

**People: We come with joy to laugh and sing,
 to remember that love is stronger than death.**

Leader: We come to celebrate the power of resurrection,
  even when all hope seems lost.
  Christ is risen!

All: Christ is risen indeed! Alleluia!

Opening Prayer

The worship leader offers a version of the opening prayers in *Calling on God*.

Hymn

Word for the Children

The word for the children is based on the lectionary readings for the week and offered by a member of the informal group that coordinates our Sunday School.

Silence

The silence is normally at least two minutes; it is held by the worship leader.

PRAYERS

Common Confession and Assurance

The confession and assurance are written by Celebration Circle for the season. Following the initial prayer, the worship leader invites prayers from the congregation "aloud and in silence," and holds the space until there is a sense that all who wish to pray aloud have offered their prayers.

When it seems that no one else wants to pray aloud, the leader offers the assurance. Here is an example of a confession and assurance from the Easter season:

Leader: Holy One, even as we celebrate
  the resurrection of your chosen one,
  we remain skeptical.

**People: We confess that we often do not believe
  that we are newly born into living hope.**

Leader: We seek to live in the power
  of imagination, myth, and dreams.

**People: But usually we cling
  to what we see, know, and experience,
  afraid to trust the reality beyond our knowing.**

Leader: When goodness, beauty, and love
  seem too much to hope for,
  we forget to rely on your promised deliverance.

**All: Holy One, hear our prayers, forgive us,
   and restore us to the joy of your salvation.**

(allow time for congregants to pray aloud)

Leader: In the risen Christ,
   God's mercy triumphs over sin and death.
   Through Jesus's name we receive
   forgiveness of all our sins.

All: Amen.

Prayers of Thanksgiving and Intercession

Following the prayers of confession and assurance, the worship leader offers an introductory prayer that speaks of situations throughout the world, the community, and within the congregation for which to give thanks and praise to God. This bidding prayer invites further prayers of thanksgiving and praise from the congregation.

When there is a sense that all who wish to pray aloud have done so, the worship leader offers another bidding prayer inviting the congregation into a time of petition and intercession. These prayers inviting the congregation's participation are found in *Calling on God*.

Prayer of Commitment

When the congregation falls silent after the prayers of thanksgiving and intercession, the worship leader may say something like, "Gathering all of our prayers into one, let us join in the prayer of commitment." The following community prayer is inspired by the Lord's Prayer and the members' commitment statement of Seekers Church:

> O Holy One, we come today
>   to claim our relationship with you.
>
> We pray for the commitment to grow together,
>   sharing the gifts you give us with others
>   here and in the wider world.
>
> Forgive us for the hurt we have inflicted,
>   and help us forgive those who have hurt us.
>
> Give us strength and discipline
>   to nurture our relationship with you;
>   to care for every part of your creation;
>   to foster justice and be in solidarity with those in need;
>   to work to end all war, and violence, and discord;
>   and to respond joyfully when you call,
>   freely giving ourselves as you have shown the way.
>
> We open our hearts to you and your creation
>   in the name of Jesus, who is the Christ. Amen.

Hymn

THE WORD

Scripture

The reading of the lectionary scriptures for the week is offered by different members of the community.

Sermon

The sermon is offered by a different individual (or group) each week, and is based on the lectionary scriptures for the week and the experience of the preacher.

Silent Reflection

The worship leader holds the silence as the congregation reflects on the sermon.

Offering

COMMUNION

We generally celebrate Communion on the first Sunday of every month, as well as on Easter Sunday. On those Sundays, a special order of worship is inserted into the worship folders. Most of the Communion liturgy remains the same from season to season, but the Great Thanksgiving portion, in which we give thanks to God for some aspect of the divine presence in creation, the life and work of Jesus, the action of the Holy Spirit, and for the church as the risen body of Christ, is written by Celebration Circle for each season.

Preparation

Leader 1: This is the table of the Heavenly Feast,
  the joyful celebration of the people of God.

Leader 2: We gather now as one body, joined around the table.
  Here we celebrate God's presence among us
  united in Christ's spirit, broken and whole all at once.

All: Nourished and hungry, loved and loving,
  sinner and forgiven;
  we make one circle of knowing,
  believing, rejoicing, being,
  as God lights and rests among us.

Great Thanksgiving

Leader 1: Holy Maker of living hope, we give you thanks for life,
  for dreams and memories that help us stand together
  in the face of grief and loss.

All: We give you thanks for your Holy Spirit,
  filling us with laughter
  as we learn to live and love anew.

Leader 2: We give you thanks for your Holy Child, Jesus,
  whose life and death and resurrection
  raise hope beyond experience.

**All: We give you thanks for your holy church,
  with steady roots and open flowers of hope,
  calling us to be your body here and now,
  in new, surprising, hopeful ways.**

Blessing the Elements

Leader 1: Christ invites everyone to eat the bread of life,
  to drink the cup of the new covenant.

Leader 2: Jesus said, *I am the bread of life.*
  You who come to me shall never hunger,
  You who believe in me shall never thirst.

Leader 1: On the night of his arrest, Jesus took bread,
  and after giving thanks to God, broke it and said,
  This is my body,
  broken for the healing of the world.
  Whenever you eat it, do so remembering me.

Leader 2: After supper, Jesus took the cup and said,
  This is the cup of the new covenant,
  poured out for you and for all.
  Whenever you drink it, do so remembering me.

**All: O Holy One, send down your Spirit
  that these gifts of bread and cup
  may be for us the body and blood of Christ.
  Unite us with Christ forever
  and bring us with the whole creation
  to your eternal realm.**

Share the Elements

If anyone does not wish to receive the elements, they are welcome to join the circle and allow the elements to pass, or remain in their seats. We serve grape juice in our cups.

Prayer of Thanksgiving and Dedication

**All: God of abundance and mercy,
  we give joyful thanks
  for your eternal love and healing presence
  in our celebration of bread and cup.
  Bless this body of Christ
  that we may attend faithfully**

to our call to be your servants,
with each other and throughout the world.
Amen.

RESPONDING IN FAITH

Shared Reflections

After Communion or the sermon, there is an opportunity for anyone present to offer their own reflections on the scripture lessons for the week or their response to worship.

Announcements

The worship leader invites members of the community to share announcements about events of interest to the community.

Hymn

Benediction

We close our worship with a blessing meant to remind all of us that we are among God's beloved, welcomed into the body of the risen Christ, and sent forth to respond to God's call to love and serve God's creation. The benedictions in the worship of Seekers Church are written by the Celebration Circle as part of the seasonal liturgy. We use the same benediction for the six to eight weeks of a liturgical season. Here is a sample Easter-season benediction, when the worship theme was "Living Hope":

> Leader: Let us go forth from this place
>   leaving the empty tomb behind.
>   Let us tell again the ancient saving stories
>   and celebrate the triumph of love over death,
>   hope over fear, joy over sadness.
>   Be the good news that Christ has risen indeed!

All: Alleluia! Amen.

The Visual Environment for Worship

As Celebration Circle writes and edits prayers for the services, we also address the question of the visual environment. As you prepare for worship each Sunday, we encourage you to consider how the language of the prayers might be enhanced through artwork, lighting, and meaningful arrangements of various objects.

At Seekers Church, we print copies of the order of worship for all the Sundays of a given season. The covers for these bulletins are imaginatively designed to complement the liturgical theme, and are made by Celebration Circle or other members of the congregation. Original artwork by adults or children is frequently used and kept for reuse in subsequent years. Sometimes this artwork is created by a single individual; other times it is the result of a communal exercise in collaborative art making. In either case the bulletin covers are a strong visual and tactile reminder of the values of creative energy and interdependence held by this community.

While it is sometimes altered for special events, the arrangement of the worship room remains substantially the same from week to week and season to season—the chairs form a rough semicircle, leaving an aisle from the central entrance doors to the altar table. A rough-hewn wooden cross—made especially for the space by a member of Seekers Church from a cherry tree that had been cut down in the yard of another member—hangs on a curved wooden partition wall. There is also an altar table and a small wooden lectern made from cherry wood in the same style as the cross. Other than windows on the walls adjacent to the cross and a net to which people sometimes attach small photographs or other objects symbolizing situations needing prayer, the second-floor room is very plain.

A processional cross and congregational banner made by other members of the community are usually present somewhere in the room as well, but the table with the cross above it is the primary visual focus during worship. As a way of both symbolically and literally laying our lives at the foot of the cross, the table may hold anything from boxing gloves to artists' manikins or a basket of summer fruit in addition to the usual candles and Communion elements. Sometimes fabric, flowers, or other objects also hang from the ceiling, fill the windowsills, or are attached to the cross, creating a visual environment that embraces the entire congregation.

As we do with the textual portion of the liturgy, the members of Celebration Circle brainstorm to arrive at images and symbols to be used as a visual analogue to the words of the liturgy. We work with the theme for the season, the portions of the text already written, and go back to the lectionary readings for inspiration. Sometimes one person will have a flash of insight and others will add details until everyone feels that it is "right." Much of this conversation is theological, as we wrestle with the implications and nuances of textures, shapes, colors, and objects.

Once the basic elements of the visual arrangement are decided, we delegate one or two people to obtain or make what is needed. Because our worship space is used for many different events by many groups, all the parts are assembled before worship each Sunday and afterward put away for the next week. Sometimes some detail is deliberately changed from week to week, but even when this is not so, the visual environment looks a little different each time than it did the week before. While often one person takes on the main responsibility for these temporary art installations, others make suggestions or changes.

While there are no limits to imagination, there are some considerations that need to be taken into account when designing seasonal additions to the visual environment. For instance, objects on or near the altar need to be large enough to be seen from the back row, but not so large that they get in the way of those who are leading worship or obscure the Communion elements or other items that are important to the particular congregation. The shape of the room will also affect how things are perceived—in a long, narrow room, everything will be seen from the same angle, while in a wide room or where worship is in the round, the installation needs to make sense from multiple viewing angles.

Generally speaking, simple is best, unless what you want to convey is a sense of clutter. We often try to maintain continuity from one season to the next, sometimes carrying elements from Lent over into the Easter season but changing them in some way. Alternatively, making a radical change at the start of a new season signals to the congregation that something is different even before a single word is spoken.

One of the things that makes our work a little easier is that we have an extensive "prop closet"—a storage room with many different kinds of fabric, candle holders, baskets, rocks, and many other odd things that we have collected over time. We also look for suitable items at home, scour thrift shops and craft stores, and bring things home from our travels that find their way into the worship space at one time or another. It also helps to have a budget, because often the image or idea that you want to convey requires a specific color of fabric that you don't happen to have, or some other item that none of you ever thought of before.

The main ingredients, however, are a lively imagination, a willingness to try anything, and a reasonably good sense of design. After all, whatever you do, it's only for a season. In a few weeks you get to do something else entirely new.

CREATING LITURGIES COLLABORATIVELY

The liturgies used at Seekers Church are created anew each season by a small group called Celebration Circle, which guides and organizes our worship. Numbering at any given time from three to seven members, Celebration Circle is part accountability group and part committee. It is one of several mission groups that serve as places of deeper belonging, in which church members live out their commitments to mission as an expression of their outward journey; to the communal life of the church; and to spiritual growth, or the inward journey.

Celebration Circle is committed to deep personal sharing, mutual trust, and collaboration as the method by which it approaches its work. Celebration Circle meets weekly for two hours. Each meeting includes a brief time for worship followed by personal sharing, the exchange of written spiritual reports, coordinating the details of upcoming worship and working on the liturgy for the next season.

OUR COLLABORATIVE PROCESS

In order to maintain a flexible but familiar framework for the worship of the community, Celebration Circle is committed to collaboration as a guiding principle. In practice, this collaboration may take many forms and occurs on many different levels. A typical sequence is as follows:

Several times a year, we think together about themes for the coming seasons. All members of the group read the lections for each of the seasons to be considered, in order both to familiarize themselves with the texts and to find some common image or idea to give focus to the season. At the next meeting, the images and ideas are shared and discussed and new ideas grow out of a brainstorming process in which no thought is rejected as being too silly or disrespectful. These sessions often are marked by playful high spirits and laughter, alternating with somber moments when we are touched at a deep level. Eventually, there is a moment when we hear as one, when it is apparent that not only the theme but the words have been found to express the way that this year's Advent, for instance, differs from any other year's. Generally we work on a single season at a time. However, sometimes the themes for an entire festal cycle—such as the period that begins with Advent and ends with the Feast of the Epiphany, or the one that begins with Ash Wednesday and carries through Lent and Easter until the Feast of Pentecost—may emerge in one session.

Once the theme for a season has been found, we look for a short reading as a meditative focus. Referred to as a "reflection paragraph," this short piece of poetry or other excerpt from theological, spiritual, or devotional writings appears at the beginning of the seasonal worship bulletin. As group members read their suggestions aloud, ideas are generated for other parts of the liturgy. Sometimes, there is disagreement, suggestions for editorial changes, or even a consensus that we need to keep looking and come back the following week with new ideas. More often, however, the right reflection paragraph seems obvious to everyone, as if the Holy Spirit has been whispering in all our ears.

At this point, a number of different things may happen. Very occasionally, one person may be inspired to write the entire liturgy based on all the ideas and images that have emerged in the conversations on theme and will bring it to the group for comments and suggestions. Generally, however, various individuals volunteer to write one or more sections and bring them back to the next meeting. Liturgies written for the current season in other years are sometimes consulted, and occasionally a section or two, or even an entire liturgy, will be reused as is, or with some minor modification. As is true for the reflection paragraph, ideas for liturgy may come from a variety of sources, including hymn texts, denominational books of worship, time-honored prayers of the church universal, inspirational writings from other traditions, or the original writings of members of the community.

When the various parts of the liturgy are written, they are printed out in the proper order and read aloud, one person taking the part of the leader and the others that of the congregation. This allows us to hear any clumsiness of language, find any tongue-twisters, and discuss the finer theological points of one phrasing or another. If there is enough time, there may be two or more read-throughs in successive weeks, allowing for further refinements of both language and typography.

COLLABORATION AND THEOLOGY

Collaboration is the practical working out of a theology in which the definition of the priesthood of all believers includes such concepts as shared leadership, Christian servanthood, and authority at the point of one's gift. This is a very demanding way of working. For those who are used to writing or art making as a solitary endeavor—the outpouring of an individual intellect and soul—it is a discipline that takes some getting used to. Collaboration requires putting one's best efforts at the service of the group and a willingness to let go of those best efforts when it is clear that something else is needed.

The difference between collaboration and creation by committee is not unlike that between *sense of the meeting*, as it is practiced by the Religious Society of Friends (Quakers), and *consensus* as it is practiced in many secular organizations. In Barry Morely's booklet "Beyond Consensus," he discusses how decisions are made among Quakers as they come to agree on the "sense of the meeting." He says that consensus

> is achieved through a process of reasoning in which reasonable people search for a satisfactory decision.... Through consensus we decide it; through sense of the meeting we turn it over, allowing it to be decided. "Reaching consensus is a secular process," says a Friend. "In sense of the meeting God gets a voice."[1]

Similarly, whether writing liturgy or designing the visual environment or deciding on the image for the bulletin cover, the members of Celebration Circle do not seek to impose their wills upon one another or to convince one another of the rightness of their idea. We do not automatically assume that the person with specialized training or talent in poetry, music, or art will have

---

1. Barry Morley, "Beyond Consensus: Salvaging Sense of the Meeting," Pendle Hill Pamphlet 307 (Wallingford PA: Pendle Hill Publications, 1993), 5.

the best solution. We do assume that those with specialized training or talent will put their gifts at the service of all, and often it is the case that a person with particular skills will offer to make something that has been envisioned by another. Our collaboration includes not only one another, but God.

It is deeply humbling to work in this way. When collaboration works—as it does surprisingly often—we are aware of the presence of the Holy Spirit in our midst, of God's gift of grace in our common life. It is this gift that we offer back into the larger community as the weekly liturgy—the work of the people.

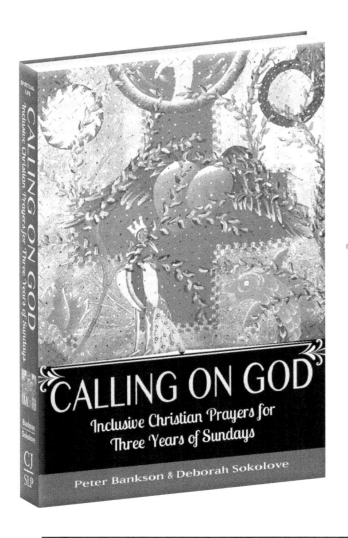

Purchase

CALLING ON GOD

Inclusive Christian Prayers for
Three Years of Sundays

for your congregation
or leadership team.

6 x 9, 400 pp, Paperback
978-1-59473-568-4 **$18.99**

Buy multiple copies of this book & save!

5–25 • 20% | 26–50 • 30%
51–174 • 35% | 175–299 • 40%
300–499 • 45% | 500+ • 50%

For more information, contact us at
(802) 457-4000 or sales@skylightpaths.com.

Christian  Journeys

FROM SKYLIGHT PATHS® PUBLISHING

Sunset Farm Offices, Route 4, P.O. Box 237, Woodstock, VT 05091
Tel: (802) 457-4000 Fax: (802) 457-4041
www.skylightpaths.com
www.christianjourneysbooks.com

Peter Bankson and **Deborah Sokolove** have been guiding people to connect with God in authentic, soul-satisfying ways for many years in their roles at Seekers Church in Washington, DC.

Peter Bankson has been a popular preacher, regular presider at worship and spiritual guide for Seekers Church since the mid-1980s. Formerly a colonel in the U.S. Army, he is now a member of the Servant Leadership Team and the mission groups that support worship and the ministry of place. He also experiments as a fiber sculptor, combining mathematical equations and sculptural crochet.

Deborah Sokolove writes and teaches on the relationship between the arts, culture and religious traditions. She is director of the Henry Luce III Center for the Arts and Religion at Wesley Theological Seminary, where she also serves as professor of art and worship. She is the author of *Sanctifying Art: Inviting Conversation between Artists, Theologians, and the Church* and has contributed articles to *Image, Call to Worship* and *The Arts in Religious and Theological Studies*. Her paintings have been shown around the country, appearing in many collections. Within Seekers Church, she serves on the worship planning group, frequently preaching and leading worship.

"A rich treasury.... All will find an invitation to congregational intercession that is at once comprehensive and concretely real."
—**Rev. Taylor W. Burton-Edwards**,
director of worship resources,
the General Board of Discipleship of
the United Methodist Church

"These prayers give us the right words to remember who we are, who God is, and the nature of the journey we are on together.... They help us reconnect with what matters most."
—**Kayla McClurg**,
author, *Passage by Passage:
A Gospel Journey*; facilitator, *inward/outward*

Other Leadership Resources from SkyLight Paths

Change and Conflict in Your Congregation (Even If You Hate Both)
How to Implement Conscious Choices, Manage Emotions and Build a Thriving Christian Community
By Rev. Anita L. Bradshaw, PhD
Positive, relational strategies and theological perspectives for navigating change and channeling conflict into a stronger sense of community and deeper understanding of one another.
6 x 9, 200 pp (est), Paperback, 978-1-59473-578-3

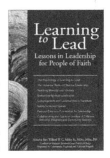

She Lives! *Sophia Wisdom Works in the World*
By Rev. Jann Aldredge-Clanton, PhD
Fascinating narratives of clergy and laypeople who are restoring sacred value to women and girls through Divine Feminine language and imagery in pursuit of just and equal faith communities.
6 x 9, 320 pp, Paperback, 978-1-59473-573-8

Women, Spirituality and Transformative Leadership: *Where Grace Meets Power*
Edited by Kathe Schaaf, Kay Lindahl, Kathleen S. Hurty, PhD, and Rev. Guo Cheen
Inspiring visions of personal leadership and powerful collaborative action. Explores the challenges and opportunities on the frontier of women's spiritual leadership.
6 x 9, 288 pp, Paperback, 978-1-59473-548-6

Learning to Lead: *Lessons in Leadership for People of Faith*
Edited by Rev. Willard W. C. Ashley Sr., MDiv, DMin, DH
Tools, advice, practical methodologies and case studies on how to help clergy and laypeople learn to do theology in context and grow into faith leadership roles.
6 x 9, 384 pp, Hardcover, 978-1-59473-432-8

CHRISTIAN JOURNEYS
FROM SKYLIGHT PATHS® PUBLISHING
Sunset Farm Offices, Route 4, P.O. Box 237, Woodstock, VT 05091
Tel: (802) 457-4000 Fax: (802) 457-40041
www.skylightpaths.com
www.christianjourneysbooks.com

Insights and Ideas for Planning Worship Using *Calling on God*

A guide to using *Calling on God* in worship communities, with:

- A sample order of service
- Suggestions for enhancing the visual environment for worship
- Guidelines for creating liturgies collaboratively in your own worship community

---

About *Calling on God: Inclusive Christian Prayers for Three Years of Sundays*

This special prayerbook is for today's Christians who find comfort in the rhythm of the traditional lectionary but long to connect with God in ways that are satisfying to the modern heart and mind. Founded on creativity, inclusivity and sharing, it encourages us to remember the divine elements of the natural world around us as we express our hopes and fears for others and ourselves. Inspiring words help us give thanks for human inventions and lament the evils of poverty, violence and oppression of all kinds while remaining mindful of God's promises of healing for a broken world.

Following the annual procession of the seasons with prayers that are appropriate for personal devotion as well as for use in leading worship, these new ways to call on God will feed your soul and inspire you to find your own fresh language for thanksgiving, praise, intercession and petition, whether in your community or personal spiritual life.

Praise for *Calling on God: Inclusive Christian Prayers for Three Years of Sundays*

"Beautiful, fresh language for Christians of all denominations.... These prayers can enrich our worship, transforming our hearts and—ultimately—strengthening our world."
— **Rev. Canon Jan Naylor Cope**, vicar, Washington National Cathedral

"Beautifully written.... An inspiring gift to all those who gather weekly to shape and sustain themselves as God's faithful people."
— **Rev. Wesley Granberg-Michaelson**, general secretary emeritus, Reformed Church in America

"In plain but powerful words, [this book] says exactly just what we all would want to say to God."
— **Bishop Eugene Taylor Sutton**, Episcopal Diocese of Maryland

"[A] rich collection.... Bring[s] human need before God in a poignant and compassionate way. Growing out of the life of one church, this book will bless many."
— **Ruth Duck, ThD**, professor of worship, Garrett-Evangelical Theological Seminary

"A powerful, prayerful, extremely useful worship aid [for] progressive congregations of many denominations and small-base communities alike.... Browse the table of contents when you need just the right prayer for many occasions."
— **Diann L. Neu**, cofounder and codirector of the Women's Alliance for Theology, Ethics and Ritual (WATER); coeditor, *New Feminist Christianity: Many Voices, Many Views*

CHRISTIAN JOURNEYS

FROM SKYLIGHT PATHS® PUBLISHING
Woodstock, Vermont
www.skylightpaths.com
www.christianjourneysbooks.com

Printed in the USA
CPSIA information can be obtained
at www.ICGtesting.com
JSHW052001150824
68134JS00059B/2753